MY

DIVINE

CONNECTION

MY DIVINE CONNECTION

FIFTY STEPS TO YOUR
DIVINE FULFILLMENT ON EARTH

৵

A self-exploratory guide for developing and strengthening
your relationship with the Divine

৵

Diego Berman PhD

Copyright © 2017 by Diego Berman

Cover design: Les Solot

All rights reserved. No part of this book may be reproduced or transmitted in any form or by any means whatsoever without express written permission from the author, except in the case of brief quotations embodied in critical articles and reviews. Please refer all pertinent questions to the publisher, Diego Berman (facebook.com/FindYourTrueNorth). This publication is for entertainment purposes only. The author of the book, Diego E. Berman, does not dispense medical advice nor prescribe the use of any technique as a form of treatment for physical or medical problems without the advice of a health practitioner or physician, either directly or indirectly. The intent of the author is only to offer information of a general nature to help you in your quest for emotional and spiritual well-being. The information presented here – as with any outside information – should be viewed as seed material for contemplation only. In the event you use any of the information in this book for yourself, which is your constitutional right, the author and the publisher assume no responsibility for your actions.

To the Divine

To my Teacher

To my loving and supportive Family

And to all of you who are embarking into your Divine Journey

ॐ

Table of Contents

PREFACE iii

INTRODUCTION v

THE FIFTY STEPS 1

HOW TO WORK WITH THIS BOOK 5

THE MESSAGES 11

    LEVEL 1 (MESSAGES 50-41) 13

    LEVEL 2 (MESSAGES 40-31) 37

    LEVEL 3 (MESSAGES 30-21) 61

    LEVEL 4 (MESSAGES 20-11) 85

    LEVEL 5 (MESSAGES 10-1) 109

AFTERWORD 133

ABOUT THE AUTHOR 135

Preface

Have you ever wanted to experience a meaningful connection with All That Is? Have you ever felt the need to explore profoundly the multifaceted aspects of your Divinity within?

Each of us follows a unique path to connect with the Divine. There are as many paths to the Divine as souls inhabiting the Earth. Honoring your unique path is the first step to strengthen your Divine Connection.

Fully designed in partnership with the Divine, this book is a non-denominational self-exploratory guide that can take you closer to your unique individual path, towards your Divine Connection. Through a series of fifty self-inquiry steps, this manual will take you on a vibrational journey, from the more physical and tangible expressions of Divinity to the highest energy frequencies of Oneness. As you discover your own personal way to connect with the Divine, you become a more conscious spark of Light and conduit of Divine expression on Earth. I invite you to join me on this journey, a journey designed for everyone who wants to be a part of Humanity's ascension into Love and Divine understanding.

Introduction

Do you know what you are?
You are a manuscript of a Divine letter.
You are a mirror reflecting a noble face.
This universe is not outside of you.
Look inside yourself;
everything that you want,
you are already that.
 —Rumi (13th Century Sufi poet)

This book was written and designed with the purpose of assisting you to develop and strengthen your connection and relationship with Divinity. Humanity has been interested in the connection with the Divine and spiritual realms ever since the dawn of civilization. In our history on this planet, thousands of groups and organizations have been created to bring the Divine into each person's life. However, each person's story is unique, and although we all have the fact of a Divine Connection in common, each of us has their own personal relationship with the Divine and their individual pathway to get there. No two people or souls are alike, nor is their connection to the Divine. Your Divine Connection is uniquely YOURS.

You and I, and everyone you see are an expression of Divine Light. But to become fully conscious of this light and to express our multidimensional Divinity at its fullest in our physical world, we need to become aware of our existing Divine Connection. Developing and understanding your personal connection with the Divine will not only allow you to open up your communication channels to the higher vibrational realms, but will also allow you to reach a more fulfilling place in life, achieving your maximum human potential and life purpose here on Earth.

The soul of each person is always connected to God, the Universe, the Source, the Creator, that everlasting, all-encompassing, and unconditional loving Energy that sustains all. However, as the soul incarnates into our physical body vehicles, and we grow up as individuals into adulthood and we experience physical life on Earth, our connection to the Source can become distorted and in some extreme cases severely blocked. An imaginary state of separation is then created, and we feel isolated, disempowered, and needing to fight for survival. It is in these circumstances that we become 'locked' into the low vibrational states of fear and pain.

The solution? Embark on a personal vibrational journey - a journey that will help us comprehend and release the low vibrations of suffering and separation as we travel along to our destination: our Divine Connection.

* * *

I would say I was a 'late bloomer' with respect to my own Divine Connection. I grew up in a home where we used to place a Jewish Star of David decorative ornament atop the Christmas tree. We used to observe both Christian and Jewish holidays, something that turned out to be very confusing to me. My friends were going to Sunday school at church and I was going to the synagogue. Even though my parents never imposed any particular religious belief system on me, I felt overwhelmed and at times uncomfortable by all the rituals on both sides.

It was then, in a moment of inner conflict, when I was about twelve years old, that I said to myself: 'I've had enough of this; I'm going to find my own path. I'm going to study the reality of life myself'. Needless to say, my parents then became the ones confused now! But fortunately, they were very understanding and accepted my decision. As a child, what I really meant by 'reality itself' was, of course, the tangible and material aspects of the physical world. I wanted to distance myself as far as I could from the veneration of something 'unseen', and at that time incomprehensive to me.

That is when I started walking my own path, by immersing myself in the study of physical sciences. Through the years, I obtained degrees in chemistry, biology and genetics, and a Ph.D. in Neuroscience. Later on, I would become an Assistant Professor of Pathology and Cell Biology at a renowned university.

However, in parallel to my scientific studies, my questions and search for a deeper meaning beyond physicality continued. This pursuit for the understanding of reality took me through the years into the practice of Buddhist meditation, yoga, and then into the study of energy healing and other subtle energy balancing modalities. My journey into the Divine has been in progress for more than three decades, with no end in sight.

Life moves in circles. What I had strongly rejected as a child called me back as an adult. I have enjoyed every moment of this journey, with its ups and downs, its detours and stops. I am infinitely grateful for all the signs and Assistance that the Divine has placed in front of me during all these years. As the saying goes; "sometimes it's the journey that teaches you a lot about your destination." And everything happens in Divine timing for each of us.

* * *

This guide you are now holding in your hands has grown in part out of my journey to discover my Divine Connection. The goal of this book is to help you identify blockages or issues you can cleanse in order to restore and strengthen your Divine Connection. As you become more aware of your own Divine Connection, you will begin to bring in more Light into your life, resulting in more optimism, well-being, and love—for yourself and others—throughout the full spectrum of your life.

For those already in touch with their Divine Connection, the messages in this guide can serve as reminders that will make your Connection stronger. Furthermore, taking the journey through this book will give you many ideas on how to explore your Divine Connection more deeply.

You can envision this book as a positive, loving, and safe guidance system that anyone can use to guide their relationship with the Divine. The concept and the messages have been developed in partnership with the Divine itself, and as such, the messages carry within them a particular type of coded energy. As you work with these messages, step by step, please allow them to help you uncover your own personal journey towards your unique Divine Connection.

The Fifty Steps

There are fifty steps, or messages, in this book. Each message has a number and a title, along with a guided self-inquiry - short questions designed to assist in further understanding and in exploring how each message might be relevant to you.

The steps are divided into five levels - ten steps per level. Each level represents a different vibrational state within the multi-dimensional spectrum of Divine expression in our physical and non-physical reality.

This five level structure serves as a roadmap that provides a clear sequence of steps for your journey. In truth, the Divine and its energetic manifestations exist in a vibrational continuum, all happening at the same time. It is the focus of our attention that determines the vibrations you experience at any given moment.

Your Divine journey will take you through the following five levels on a continuous ascending vibrational adventure, one step at a time:

Level 1, Messages 50-41: External and societal factors that might be affecting your connection to the Divine. The first group of messages focuses on our daily physical needs and those activities influenced by our relationships with other human beings and the institutions that society has created. These are issues that belong mostly to the Earthly plane and our human interactions with the physical world. In energetic terms, they represent the lower densities, the material and fundamental root aspects of our life on Earth.

Level 2, Messages 40-31: Personal factors you might need to focus on to open up your Divine communication. The second level focuses on issues that we encounter on our journey to self-awareness and personal identity. They are intrinsically linked to our emotional relationship with ourselves, others, and the Divine. Energetically speaking, these messages vibrate at higher frequencies than the ones in the previous level, since they are mostly related to the mind, not the body.

Level 3, Messages 30-21: The interface between Divinity and your own energy, your hopes, and dreams. The third group of messages represents the union of our human individual mind and the Divine mind. It is here that the Divine expresses itself through us to the physical world. It is the perfect balance of human and Divine partnership enacting your life purpose on Earth. This is the 'in the zone' area, the sweet spot, the 'aha!' moments, in which Divine guidance can result in practical actions taken by us on the physical plane.

Level 4, Messages 20-11: The different channels Divinity can employ to communicate with us. The fourth group of messages addresses the ways in which the non-physical aspects of the Divine communicate with the physical planes and particularly with you. These varied Divine communication channels can take several shapes and forms, and you will most likely resonate with a few of them. It is here that our relationship with the Divine finds its preferred 'radio channel' for communication. These messages contain vibrations much higher than our physical human experience, since they originate in non-physical planes beyond our physical senses.

Level 5, Messages 10-1: The attributes of the Divine itself. The last group of messages puts us in touch with the ever-lasting qualities of Divinity. Although it is almost impossible to put into words and describe this immense and all-encompassing creative Energy, these messages will help you translate some of its qualities into human terms and emotions. These are messages that correspond to the highest vibrations within the five groups since they originate way beyond our physical plane. Even though we can experience them at our human level, they come from the purest states of universal Energy creation.

Now let's get started and learn how to work with these messages.

How to work with this book

You can work with this book in one of two ways.

The first is the 'Classic Approach', in which you read the book as any other book, from beginning to end. The second way, the 'Intuitive Approach', is more unstructured and interactive. Both will be explained in detail below.

I suggest you start with the Classic Approach so you can become familiar with the meaning and energy of each message. In this way, as you move from message to message, you will be developing a deeper sense of self-awareness, helping you to focus your attention into each different Divine aspect of your life.

As you journey through the book, you might start noticing synchronicities in your life, events that appear out of the blue, giving you ideas, insights, and helping you reconnect with your Divine within. Please pay attention to these events, for they will be coming into your awareness for specific purposes. Remember, the Divine is constantly communicating with us.

The Classic Approach

Before you begin, find a quiet place and time during the day when you won't be disturbed. If you need to, turn your cell phone and TV off so you can be fully present on this work.

Start your Divine journey by reading the messages in a consecutive order, from level 1 up to level 5. Study each step and follow the questions provided below each message as guides for your own self-exploration or short meditations. It is important that you listen to your intuition as you read the messages. Explore how each message specifically applies to your own life, either in the past or the present. Once you feel you have spent enough time assimilating and understanding a message, you can move forward to the next.

It would be useful to keep a journal (either in paper or digital form) to write down your feelings, insights, or any other type of sensations that come to you when studying each message. Feel free to also write down your thoughts directly on the back of the page devoted to each message.

Focus on only one level (ten steps) per day, no more than that. The reason is to focus your awareness and energy vibrations at one level at a time. By doing this, you will have time to incorporate the new vibrations more efficiently without mixing the vibrations of two different levels. If you want to go deeper into each message and obtain further insights and benefits, then I suggest you take your journey at a much slower pace, working on one message per day. In this way, your complete journey through the book will take you fifty days.

If you find that along the way a particular message strongly resonates with you and elicits any feelings of guilt, shame, or regret, please do not judge yourself. Allow yourself to experience these feelings, let them flow through you, and then use them as tools, or stepping stones, to understand why and how those issues might be affecting your Divine Connection. Remember, this book is in your hands so that you and the Divine can become 'closer' friends. In truth, this loving Connection has been, is, and always will be there, with and in you. The aim of this journey is to help you to re-Connect.

At the end of each level, you will find a page to highlight the top three messages that resonated most with you on that particular level.

After you have fully journeyed through the book you will have a renewed sense of how your Divine Connection plays a role in your life and how a deeper Connection can literally create miracles for you and those around you. You will also have a stronger sense of the unique ways in which the Divine is expressed in you and through you into the world.

The Intuitive Approach

The Intuitive Approach is an interactive way of working with this book. You through your intuition will decide which of the fifty messages to read next.

The approach is based on the intrinsic vibration of numbers. In Western Pythagorean numerology, each number, or combination of numbers, holds a specific vibration. But worry not, you do not need to have any background on numerology to use this Intuitive approach, which I hope you will find very easy and fun to use, as you will see below. Again, I suggest that you start with the Classic Approach and then move into the Intuitive approach.

This Intuitive Approach is not designed to predict your future but rather to bring your awareness into those aspects of your Divine Connection that need to be uncovered in a particular situation. Once these have been identified and aligned, you will find yourself in a vibrational space conducive to productive manifestations and positive outcomes.

The Law of Attraction is a universal law by which we attract similar experiences to ourselves depending on our mental or emotional vibrational states. By using this law, as you *think and focus your energy on a particular question*, you will be intuitively guided to the message(s) that holds the vibrations for restoring and aligning that particular issue. Here's a step-by-step description of the process:

Step 1. Think of the question or issue you want to address. You can say it to yourself or aloud or write it on a piece of paper.

Step 2. Take a deep breath, close your eyes, try to empty your mind, and center yourself in your connection with the Divine, or simply connect with your Heart.

Step 3. Now use your intuition by sensing which number, from 1 to 50, comes into your mind or resonates with the question you posed on Step 1. You may receive or visualize just one number or more. No number or message is an accident or mistake, since you are tuning your own vibration (while asking the question) to the vibrations of the messages in this book.

Step 4. Once you pick your number(s), refer back to the book and read the message(s) that corresponds to the number(s) you received. Even if upon reading the message its meaning makes no clear sense to you at the time or is not what you expected to see please make sure you still listen to its guidance and use the guided questions to further understand the connection of that message to you or that particular situation.

Step 5. Give thanks for the guidance you have just received.

Here are some examples of the questions you might ask:

- What issues should I focus on to open up my personal Divine Connection?
- What aspect of my Divine Connection can help improve my current situation?
- What Divine theme should I be focusing on today to simply bring in more blessings into my day? Here, you can intuitively connect with one message in the morning of each day to help you focus on a single Divine Connection theme that might appear during the day.
- For a deeper intuitive work at every level, you can select one message from each of the five different groups. In this way, you will be able to work on five specific messages at all five vibrational levels. You can use this approach once a week, and devote the seven days to connect with these five messages. You can continue using this method week after week.

You may also use this Intuitive Approach on behalf of others (with their permission), such as friends and family members, who might also want to explore the aspects of their Divine Connection in their lives.

* * *

There is no relationship of greater importance to achieve than the one between you, in your physical body and the Divinity from which you have come. If you tend to that relationship first and foremost, you will then, and only then, have the stable footing to proceed into other relationships. Your relationship with your own body, your relationship with money, your relationship with your family, the people you work with, your government, your world, will all fall swiftly and easily into alignment once you tend to this fundamental, primary Divine relationship first.

Enjoy walking this path. It is YOUR personal journey in partnership with the Divine. Walk it in peace, love, and joy. Your Divine Connection is the key that will open the doors to your own Divinity and to your maximum potential as a human being on Earth.

I'll be seeing you again on the other side of your journey with some final words.

Blessings.

The Messages

Let your Divine journey begin...

Level 1
(Messages 50-41)

∾

External and Society factors

These messages deal with issues that are generated by external situations in our lives, which then can become obstacles in the communication with the Divine.

These messages tackle our most earthly issues and hence carry the lowest energy vibrations in the book. Pay close attention to each message, as these day-to-day life situations are key to improving your connection with the Divine.

50

FINANCES

Financial issues can frequently push us towards a pure materialistic view of reality. The human ego easily uses finances as an excuse to hijack our energy away from the focus on the Divine. When in reality, our earthly needs are always Divinely orchestrated.

༄

Have financial issues ever hindered your connection to the Divine? Have you noticed an improved Divine connection once you released those economic concerns? Yes, we all do need to pay the bills, but trust the Divine will always provide if you seek with a true heart.

49

CHILDHOOD

Our relationship with the Divine can be affected by events we experienced during our childhood. These formative years, in which we develop our emotional connections to our physical parents, caregivers, and authority figures, can affect how our Divine Connection develops into our adulthood.

৯

How did your childhood experiences shape your current connection to the Divine? Do you remember specific circumstances that either created feelings of rejection, affinity, or confusion, regarding spiritual matters? Was your sense of curiosity supported and stimulated when you were a child, or were you educated in a more conservative environment?

48

FEARS

Each human being has a deep driving force that pushes them forward fearlessly no matter what external circumstances they face. This innate force is connected to your soul; it wants you to evolve, to maximize your potential, and to develop your Divine Connection.

∽

Can you recall a time in your life when you acted fearlessly, pushed by an inexplicable force that brought your life up to a better and more fulfilling place?

If so, that was a true Divine Connection moment! Are you aware now of any barriers imposed by fear that might be blocking your connection to the Divine?

47

SKEPTICISM

A healthy dose of skepticism and curiosity can be useful tools in a self-discovery and experiential journey towards the Divine. However, blind skepticism based on other people's experiences and false inferences can be a big barrier in developing our personal connection with the Divine.

༄

Have you ever turned your own skepticism into a driving force to explore and seek the Divine?

Have you ever had that 'special' experience that transformed your skepticism into 'believing' in the existence of your Divine Connection?

46

PAST-LIVES

Our relationship with the Divine can sometimes be affected by issues that go way back in our soul's history. Past-life situations, or even childhood situations, most likely traumatic ones may have shaped your current view of Divinity.

⁓

Do you feel an inexplicable connection, either rejection or affinity, to a particular type of spiritual or religious belief? If so, this could be an indication of an ancient soul memory playing a role and affecting your connection with Divinity in profound ways.

45

RELIGION

Our personal Divine Connection can be strongly shaped by the various religious belief systems our societies impose on us since birth. This might erect barriers in our heart-to-heart relationship with the Divine. The truth is only One and we will find it in our hearts in communion with the Divine.

ॐ

Have you ever felt that the organized religious system you grew up with actually impaired or improved your connection with the Divine? How did that religious system help shape your current Divine Connection?

44

JUSTICE

We live in a world where the word 'justice' can trigger a lot of emotions. As a society, we keep anger, resentment, hate, violence, in our hearts to our own detriment. We always feel entitled to do 'justice', when in fact only Divine justice and Divine order exist in the grand scheme of things. As you align yourself with your own Divine Connection, you will understand that Divine justice will always find its way.

༄

Do you think we would live in a more equalitarian and compassionate society if everyone improved their personal Divine Connection? Do you harbor any harsh feelings of injustice within you? If so, please allow yourself to release your feelings of anger and resentment to the Divine. As you do this, you are generating more love and Divine justice for all.

43

FAMILY

Often, our families play a significant role in the shaping of our Divine Connection. Family members can be supportive of our path, and other times less understanding or even be against our life's choices. Your Divine Connection is only yours to experience; we all have unique paths, make peace with this and bring understanding to your loved ones.

༄

How was your Divine Connection affected by your relationship with your family? Were your parents or other family members influential on how you relate to the Divine? Have they respected your personal spiritual choices? Are you able to respect their choices?

42

SURVIVAL

Our Divine Connection can become blurred when we are too focused on our 'survival mechanisms'. Because of our physical existence, we tend to get lost in the search for material things that we believe will help us keep going, hence forgetting that it is the generosity of the Divine itself that truly provides the relief and answers we seek.

ॐ

How much time do you spend each day thinking about 'surviving', running after your 'needs', versus thanking the Divine for what you already have and for what is to come? Do you feel that your material accumulations are enough to provide you with a fulfilling life?

41

JUDGMENT

Our societies shape our opinions, creating different types of belief systems and judgments. Instead of learning to discern, we grow up constantly judging ourselves and others. Judging becomes a barrier, a separation, and a negation of the reality of others, hence breaking down our interconnected Divine Connection.

༄

Have you found yourself judging others, or yourself, today? Where is that judgment stemming from? Do you think this judging action prevents you from seeing the Divine in others? How does judging affect your own Divine Connection?

Level 1 Assessment

After reading and working with this group of messages, what are the top three messages that most resonated with you, or that required further time, or research, to assimilate?

Please write them below.

Message _____

Message _____

Message _____

Level 2
(Messages 40-31)

ತ

Personal influences

This group depicts human personal issues that might be limiting your connection to the Divine. These issues may have developed in this lifetime or be derived from our ancestral lines. These are aspects of the Divine that shape your individual identity. Focusing on these messages will help you understand your own Self.

40

GENUINENESS

Being true to yourself is an essential component of your connection with the Divine. Your genuineness is a gift, and sharing who you really are, your authentic Self, with the world will create a sense of peace and fulfillment. The more genuine your life is, the better your Divine Connection will flow.

༄

Are there any areas in your life where you are still not fully expressing your authentic Self? What is preventing you from doing so? Do you feel you are being completely genuine even with yourself? Or do you live your life trying to imitate others?

39

HUMILITY

We often see ourselves as the 'center of the Universe'; our human ego plays this game with us constantly. This lack of humility and of interconnectedness can blind us from the Divine. Humility towards the Divine and our fellow travelers will allow you to connect with the Divine without barriers.

൭

Do you feel there is a Divine plan for each of us? How much do you feel you can truly control your life? Are you humble enough in front of the vastness and magnificence of the Universe? Do you give credit to the role of the Divine in your life?

38

HUMOR

Learning to laugh and finding the humor in ourselves, or in any situation, is part of understanding that life can be an enjoyable process, and that it does not necessarily need to be taken 'too' seriously. The Divine has a great sense of humor, so please add some to your life in order to strengthen and uplift your Divine Connection. A smile on your face is a smile in the Divine.

৶

When was the last time you truly laughed at yourself?! Have you ever felt that the Divine was being playful with you? A funny coincidence perhaps? Playfulness and humor are key aspects of the Divine! Allow yourself to be playful as a way to strengthen your Divine Connection.

37

BLESSINGS

We are constantly surrounded by blessings in our life. Most of the time, our minds and energy are focused on personal concerns and worries and we do not appreciate the millions of blessings that the Divine bestows upon us. Count your blessings indeed, no matter how big or small, for this will generate a better appreciation of your connection with the Divine.

༄

What's the hidden, or sometimes obvious, blessing in your current life situation? Have you been grateful to the Divine lately for this? How are these blessings contributing to your personal growth? Are you open to the blessings the Divine is pouring over you?

36

SELF-EXPRESSION

We are all unique individuals, and each of us brings specific attribute combinations into this world. Increasing our self-expression and being true to our inner Self is a key factor for strengthening our connection to the Divine.

॰ಲ๏

Have you lately shown the world your soul's true colors? Your inner Divine beauty? All the unique gifts you can offer the world? Your TRUE inner Light? How are you expressing your Divine spark in the world?

35

ACCEPTANCE

Accepting who you are is a key step in strengthening your connection to the Divine. Your soul chooses certain challenges for specific purposes and resisting your own path will take you away from living your true purpose. Accept your body, your gifts, and your emotions, as they are there with you to take you closer to the Divine. Love yourself as you are, and accept your beauty as you were created.

⁕

Are there any aspects of yourself that you do not yet fully accept? If so, have you asked yourself why this is so? Perhaps you have not yet realized that each human being is a spark of the Divine? And as such, that the only thing you need to feel for yourself is Love and acceptance?

34

TENDERNESS

Often, we go through life being unkind to ourselves. This ends up creating feelings of low self-esteem and low self-confidence, which prevent us from standing in our own Divine power. Allowing for more tenderness and loving kindness towards yourself on a daily basis will make that Divine Connection more caring, efficient, and uplifting. Please be gentle with your own heart, which after all it is a sparkle of the Divine within.

༄

Have you been lovingly kind and gentle to yourself today? Have you noticed any moments of self-depreciation or harsh self-judgment? Increasing your moments of tenderness and loving kindness will allow your Divine Connection to soar!

33

FORGIVENESS

Sometimes we carry with us a lot of resentment and unforgiveness. This slows us down on the path of our spiritual evolution, and creates blockages in our connection with the Divine. Forgiving yourself and others can bring amazing healing benefits for everyone involved, and more importantly, allows your Divine Connection to reach higher places.

୨

Are you still holding unforgiveness or resentment in your heart? Who or what are you still resenting? When was the last time you fully forgave? Close your eyes, ask your heart, and let it go. Your Divine Connection will thank you a thousand times.

32

HUMAN EGO

The different aspects of our personalities, driven by the human ego, can become a big challenge to our Divine connection. After all, there is no separation between us and the Divine, but the human ego constantly creates such an illusion.

ॐ

How do you calm the ego down so that the Divine can shine through? How often do you act from an ego place as opposed to a loving Divine place? Can you clearly identify when your actions are ego-driven?

31

PHYSICAL BODY

Our physical bodies are vehicles for the Divine to express itself on this physical plane, and as such, they need to be well cared for and maintained. Otherwise, the physical imbalances/dis-eases can become obstacles in our connection to the Divine. As you improve your connection with your physical body, you strengthen the link with your Divine Connection.

୶

Have you treated your body well today? What areas do you feel you would like to improve in your physical body? Diet? Exercise? Breathing work? Relaxing Self-care? Do you feel the state of your physical body influences your connection to the Divine? Do you allow the Divine to help you on your journey to physical well-being?

Level 2 Assessment

After reading and working with this group of messages, what are the top three messages that most resonated with you, or that required further time, or research, to assimilate?

Please write them below.

Message _____

Message _____

Message _____

℘

Level 3
(Messages 30-21)

༄

Hopes and Dreams

These messages act like a bridge between the Divine mind and the human mind. They depict human hopes and dreams that are usually inspired by our Divine soul's mission.

30

EVOLUTION

Our souls are constantly searching for a path towards evolution, also known as Ascension. This soul evolutionary process is non-stoppable, and it keeps pushing our human physical form towards changes and challenges that allow for that evolution to happen.

ბო

Do you feel you have moved forward lately? If so, in which area(s) of your life? Is there anything that is preventing you from reaching the next step in your life?

29

POWER & GLORY

Our Divine Connection becomes stronger once we understand that all of our hopes and dreams can only manifest into form by the Power of the Divine. It is this Divine Power and Glory that supports our human desires and existence.

∽

Have you ever wondered how much Power is needed to sustain our presence in this Universe? Have you felt this Power and Glory while looking at the stars, or into the eyes of a child?

28

JOY

Joy, a feeling of great pleasure and happiness, is one of our inner basic human characteristics. The experience of Joy takes us closer to the Divine, since the Divine itself, and the expression of its Love for us, stem from pure Joy. Be joyful, and your Divine Connection will soar.

୨

Have you lately been experiencing true Joy? What makes your heart sing with joy? Does connecting with the Divine bring you joy? Do you feel joy when you express
and receive Love?

27

LIFE PURPOSE

Each one of us has a Divine life purpose here on Earth. Everyone's purpose is equally valuable and valid, as long as you align yourself with the Divine and put your focus on how you may be of service to the big Divine plan for humanity. Living your life purpose will allow your Divine Connection to flow unrestricted.

∞

Have you ever wondered what your life purpose is? Has this search brought you closer to the Divine? How did your connection to the Divine change once you found 'your calling' in life?

26

BELIEVE

As human beings, we shape our reality according to our belief systems. Believing is the constant focusing on a particular thought. This is a natural aspect of our human mind. Believing in ourselves, in others, and in the Divine, is what propels us forward. The mere act of believing in the Divine can help you open up your Divine Connection.

∽

Have you ever questioned your own beliefs? How have they changed through the years? Are you able to identify how your beliefs have affected and shaped the way you live your life? Have your beliefs helped you, or not, in improving your Divine Connection?

25

ASCENSION

**Increasing the vibration of your body and mind is a key process in your Ascension journey. Your Divine Connection will become stronger as your whole being starts vibrating at higher frequencies closer to the Divine realms. In this way, your Divine communication becomes clearer
and more frequent.**

৩

Have you felt your whole body frequency increasing lately? Have you been feeling lighter, more connected to the Divine? And perhaps less interested in mainstream 3D low vibrational events? Have you been feeling the need to connect more and more with like-minded spiritual individuals and topics?

24

BEAUTY

The Divine also presents itself to us by manifesting beautiful things. Everywhere, in the flower that blooms, in the bird that sings, in the star that shines, in your own soul, we see reflections of Divine beauty. Find that Beauty within and around you, in your dreams and in your hopes, to strengthen your Divine Connection.

✿

What's the most beautiful thing you've ever seen or created? What's the most beautiful thing you can see right now? A familiar face? A piece of art? Your own smile? The love of a dear one? Divine beauty makes your heart shine, and it consolidates your Divine Connection.

23

FAITH

Faith is the soul-deep human trust and conviction that something is or exists. Faith in the Divine, and in its majestic power, is a key tool in the path to opening your Divine communication.

༄

Have you ever found yourself taking a 'leap of faith' in life? That deep 'trust in the Universe' that things will work out positively? Has your faith allowed you to break any inner limitations?

22

DREAMS

Human dreams and aspirations are strong forces that propel our soul to expand and develop in this physical plane. It is important that we are true to these dreams, that we follow them and trust this inner call. Taking action towards the realization of these dreams will strengthen your connection to the Divine.

॰ঽ॰

Are you taking action towards the manifestation of your dreams? Are your dreams truly yours or are they being influenced by society or peer pressure? Have you been denying or encouraging those dreams?

21

SERVICE

We all come into this world with an innate capacity to be of Service, to be of Service to the Divine and to others, which in the end is the same thing. It is when we find this Service in our lives that we become truly useful. It is your own Divine Connection that calls you into Service.

༄

Have you ever felt compelled, driven by an inner force, to assist others, to heal, to improve people's life quality? Have you ever had the sense of working for a much broader and less personal agenda? For a cause that is bigger than life itself? How can you be of Service?

Level 3 Assessment

After reading and working with this group of messages, what are the top three messages that most resonated with you, or that required further time, or research, to assimilate?

Please write them below.

Message _____

Message _____

Message _____

Level 4
(Messages 20-11)

❧

Divine communication channels

These messages depict several ways in which Divinity communicates with us. Each person has a different and preferred way(s) to interact with Divinity. These messages will help you identify the communication channel that most resonates with you at the present moment.

20

SACRED PLACE

There are Sacred Places all around the world, where specific types of Divine Energy are concentrated. These sacred places are conducive to a more fluid communication with the Divine. That said, the closest sacred place to the Divine is in your own Heart.

༶

Have you ever been to a sacred place? Was it a natural or a man-made place? Did your Divine Connection become stronger by being there? Do you consider your own heart to be a sacred place?

19

NUMBERS

The Divine can connect with us in many different ways. One of them is through the use of mathematics, the universal language of energy manifestation. Each number or number combination has a particular energy and meaning associated with it. This is a very unambiguous and clear way for the Divine to send us messages.

∽

Have you noticed any numbers that repeat themselves lately around you? Or for seemingly unknown reasons, you feel drawn to a particular number or types of numbers such as odd or even? Do you often wonder about the reason why you see certain numbers and not others?

18

DIVINE TIMING

Yet another way the Divine communicates with us is through synchronicities, by creating and attracting situations into our lives at the right moment that change our lives forever. This is called Divine Timing. If you ever experienced the famous 'being at the right place at the right time', this was your Divine Connection in action.

෴

Have you ever experienced Divine Timing in your life? Has it been an important factor in shaping your life journey? Do you allow for Divine timing to happen or do you usually wait impatiently for things to occur? Or perhaps a combination of both?

17

MEDITATION

Connecting with the Divine can take many forms and shapes. One of them is through the practice of meditation. There are many different ways to meditate. Devoting your time to developing a daily practice of meditation can help you strengthen your Divine Connection.

֍

Do you meditate? If so, how often? What's your favorite meditation modality? Sitting, walking, exercising, chanting, reading ancient texts, or any others? Do you find that meditation allows you to feel more centered and connected to the Divine?

16

WISDOM

Sometimes, the Divine whispers words of Wisdom into our hearts and minds. Divine inspiration is yet another way for Divinity to communicate directly with us and to unveil the path for our Divine and earthly human fulfillment.

༶

Have you ever had a sudden bout of inspiration? Ideas that appear out of nowhere in your mind and they feel exactly right in your heart? Revelations that change lives. That's Divine Wisdom in action.

15

MOTHER NATURE

One of the most basic ways in which the Divine communicates with us is through the Natural world. Its night and day cycles, seasons, rocks, plants, and animals, are all intrinsically connected to us. Being close to this basic type of creative energy is a wonderful way to sync yourself with your own natural rhythms and communicate with the Divine.

ல

Have you been outdoors around nature lately? Have you interacted with any plants, animals, or rocks? Have you been able to sense that Divine language within Nature itself? The wind? The sun? The moon?

14

ANGELIC BEINGS

One way the Divine communicates with us is through its Divine messengers, the Angelic beings. Angels and Archangels are non-denominational loving and peaceful non-physical energies that can act as intermediaries between us and the infinite mind of the Divine. We can all develop our personal Angelic Connection.

ა

Have you lately interacted with your Angels? Have you felt their love and support? We all have the ability to hear, see, and sense these Divine beings. Angels are here to guide us and protect us. Get in touch with your Angels for a stronger Divine Connection.

13

TEACHERS & GUIDES

The Divine also communicates with us through Teachers and Guides. Most likely, all those who seek with an honest heart will reach a stage in which the need of a Master or Guide will appear. This Teacher, either past or contemporary, will act as a catalyzer and take your Divine Connection to a higher place by opening doors within yourself. The doors will be open, but you will have to walk through them.

∽

Have you ever felt the need of a Teacher or Guide? How did your Divine Connection change after working with this Teacher? How do you feel a Guide would be helpful to your Divine Connection?

12

RELATIONSHIPS

The Divine frequently communicates with us through other people/souls that come into our lives. Our human relationships can be wonderful means for the Divine to send messages to us. These relationships can be as short as a minute, or as long as a lifetime, but in every case your Divine Connection will be changed for good.

༄

Have you ever had a relationship that made a positive contribution to your Divine Connection? Perhaps a friend? A pet? A family member? Or even a stranger? What messages did those relationships deliver?

11

PRAYER

Prayer, a request or invocation sent from our Heart to the Divine, has always been a key way of communication between us and Divinity. Prayer can take many forms, can be spoken, written, sang, or just whispered internally. Prayer is the connective tissue of your Divine Connection.

∽

How often do you pray? What's your favorite modality of praying? Do you usually pray for yourself or others? Have you experienced the benefits of praying?

Level 4 Assessment

After reading and working with this group of messages, what are the top three messages that most resonated with you, or that required further time, or research, to assimilate?

Please write them below.

Message _____

Message _____

Message _____

☙

Level 5
(Messages 10-1)

The Divine

Focusing on these messages will help you connect with the most basic and immutable qualities of the ever-lasting Energy that supports everything that exists. These are the Divine qualities that can fully strengthen your Divine Connection. They are the highest vibrational messages in the book.

10

ENLIGHTMENT

The Divine mind holds all the knowledge ever present in the Universe. It is enlightened, and it can also enlighten us. This is the very same wisdom that can connect you to All That Is and can elevate your life and alleviate suffering. Develop your Divine Connection and this wisdom will be there for you, always.

༄

Have you ever had a moment of enlightenment? That moment when you suddenly see the truth about a situation, or an idea comes to your mind that changes the course of your life? Do you usually act on those bright insights that come to you as if by 'magic'?

9

THE NOW

The Divine is constantly present in and around you. It is in the present moment, in the now, where your Divine Connection is the strongest. Not in the past, not in the future, but right now. Be mindful of your Divine Connection in the present moment and you will be connected to eternity.

∽

Where is your focus at the present moment? Are you fully mindful of this moment in time while you are reading these words? Or are your thoughts scattered? Can you place your full focus on your Divine Connection for a single moment in time?

Give it a try right now!

8

ABUNDANCE

We live in an abundant Universe. A lack of abundance is just a mere illusion and is only created by our human ego. There are limitless resources available to us, if we only allow ourselves to receive from the abundant and infinite Divine. Increase your Divine Connection and allow Heaven's gifts into your hands.

༄

What resources do you feel you are lacking? Money? Time? Health? Love? Do you think your mind and heart are fully accessible to Divine abundance? Or are you restricting yourself? The more you connect with the Divine and accept its blessings, the more you will live in its infinite Abundance.

7

LIMITLESS

The Divine can reach places that go beyond what our human minds can imagine and comprehend. Divinity is limitless, it is unbound, it is unrestricted. Allow your Divine Connection to expand and reach new places far beyond.

൞

Have you ever noticed how your awareness changes as you focus on the unlimited aspects of yourself? How does your Divine Connection help you to feel less restricted in your day-to-day life? Are there any self-limiting beliefs guiding your actions?

6

COMPASSION

Another intrinsic aspect of Divinity is compassion, compassion for every single one of its creations. Human beings are able to feel compassion for others simply because the Divine is within us all. Experiencing loving compassion for yourself and others is yet another way to strengthen your Divine Connection.

༄

When was the last time you were involved in an act of compassion? That unselfish concern for the misfortune of others? Have you ever felt that deep lovingly kind Divine compassionate connection for yourself in your own heart?

5

DIVERSITY

The power of Divine creativity is infinite. Diversity is a common theme all over the Universe, and every single creation stems from the Divine. Accepting and loving each of the diverse manifestations of the Divine will take your Divine Connection a step further.

※

Have you ever truly observed the diversity and creativity of the Divine? Have you noticed the incredible variety of Divine creations? From a shell in the ocean, to the most distant galaxy? Can you see the Divine creative force underlying each single manifestation, including yourself?

4

TRUTH

The only Path of Truth is your own Divine Connection. This Path is only yours, and has to be walked only by you in communion with the Divine. Only by knowing the Divine, you will know the Truth.

☙

Do you feel you have found your path of truth? What do you think a path of truth is about? Do you consider your Divine Connection to be a path of truth? How often do you walk this true path?

3

OMNIPRESENCE

Everything that exists, everything that is and is not, is part of and is connected to the Divine. From a blade of grass to the immensity of the cosmos, the Divine is omnipresent. Therefore, seeing Divinity in everything that surrounds you is a way to awaken and increase your Divine Connection.

༄

What do you see now? These words? This body? The room you are in? But can you see the Divine in everything you see? Can you feel that Divine Connection within
and outside of you?

2

UNCONDITIONAL LOVE

God, the Universe, Source, the Creator, the Cosmic mind, so many names for the same Unconditional Love. A Love that lives in the heart of each person, a Love without restrictions, a Divine Love that only loves.

୨୧

Love is all around us... Within us... Take a deep breath, close your eyes, and just feel this in your heart. That Energy that supports you here is Unconditional Love; get in touch with it frequently. Improve that loving connection.

1

UNITY

I AM the Divine. There is only Unity.

Once you realize there is no separation between you and the Divine, your Divine Connection naturally appears, since it is yourself connecting with yourself and the infinite Light.

୭

Do you think or feel the Divine is something separate/different from you? How do you relate to Divinity? Can you see yourself and the Divine as one?

Level 5 Assessment

After reading and working with this group of messages, what are the top three messages that most resonated with you, or that required further time, or research, to assimilate?

Please write them below.

Message _____

Message _____

Message _____

Afterword

Congratulations! You have made it to the other side of your Divine Connection journey. It is my hope that after reading and working with this book you have a better appreciation and understanding of your unique way to connect with the Divine and of the role the Divine constantly plays in your life.

Now that you have journeyed from the more tangible and day-to-day aspects of yourself into the high frequencies of Divine non-physicality, I invite you to choose five messages, one from each level, that stood out and strongly resonated with you throughout your journey. These are the main themes that delineate the way your personal Divine Connection is expressed at the present moment. In other words, these five messages illustrate the direct path that your soul has chosen at this time to find its way to, and express, the Divine within.

Use the space below to list those messages to have a more unified view of your path.

Level 1 Main message: _____

Level 2 Main message: _____

Level 3 Main message: _____

Level 4 Main message: _____

Level 5 Main message: _____

Of course, this path is not written in stone and most likely will shift as your life changes and as you continue to evolve as a human being on Earth. However, this unified view will give you a clearer picture, one that you can focus on to further deepen your Divine Connection.

After walking through the fifty steps of your Divine journey, perhaps you now have realized that you want to study a new spiritual topic of interest or that you want to engage yourself in a new project or hobby to develop certain aspects of your Divinity. All these are wonderful outcomes of your Divine Connection journey, so do follow your Heart and Divine guidance to continue expressing and enacting your Divine Connection on Earth.

Once you have completed your first reading of the book, revisit it once a year, or as often as you'd like, to check in with yourself and see where you are on your path to and with the Divine. You can always use the Intuitive Approach any day.

Your Divine journey will continue beyond the pages of this book, but always remember that these messages will be here for you any time you feel the need to find a Divine re-Connection moment.

May you continue traveling in peace, in joy, and in unity.

Blessings.

About The Author

Since early childhood, **Dr. Diego Berman** was interested in experiences that challenge the mainstream paradigms. He grew up in Buenos Aires, Argentina, where he obtained his first degree in Biology and Molecular Genetics at the University of Buenos Aires. Later he developed an interest in the brain and cognitive functions, which led him to move to Israel and pursue a Ph.D. in Neuroscience at the Weizmann Institute of Science. In 2002, Diego moved to New York City and continued his scientific work at Columbia University as an Assistant Professor, focusing on the neurobiology of Alzheimer's disease. In parallel to his academic and scientific career, Diego's personal inner journey led him into the fields of consciousness studies, Buddhist meditation, yoga, and other paths of inner contemplative practices. In 2010, Diego's first encounter with Archangel Raphael was featured in Doreen Virtue's book 'The Healing Miracles of Archangel Raphael'. Diego is a certified Nutri-Energetic Systems© practitioner, an Assertiveness

Life Coach©, and an Angel Card Reader©. Diego also speaks Light Languages, which is yet another form of vibrational energy balancing.

You can find Diego on his Facebook page at:

www.facebook.com/FindYourTrueNorth

Tools for a Joyful and Purposeful Living